HENRY FIELDING
THE TENTATIVE REALIST

*Oxford University Press, Ely House, London W.*1

GLASGOW NEW YORK TORONTO MELBOURNE WELLINGTON
CAPE TOWN SALISBURY IBADAN NAIROBI LUSAKA ADDIS ABABA
BOMBAY CALCUTTA MADRAS KARACHI LAHORE DACCA
KUALA LUMPUR HONG KONG TOKYO

HENRY FIELDING
THE TENTATIVE REALIST

By

MICHAEL IRWIN

CLARENDON PRESS
OXFORD
1967

© Oxford University Press 1967

Made and printed in Great Britain by
William Clowes and Sons, Limited, London and Beccles

To My Mother

PREFACE

One of the things I am trying to show in this book is that Fielding was a didactic writer, a moralist, from the very beginning of his literary career. The best evidence for this is the regularity with which he returns in his work to a number of specific social and ethical issues. It is the consistency and frequency, rather than the quality, of his comments on these topics that most clearly reveal his moral preoccupation. Logically, therefore, I should have begun this book with a massive, thickly-illustrated chapter demonstrating chronologically the persistence of the relevant themes. Since this promised to be very dull I chose instead to risk a methodological loop. My comparatively brief account of the ideas in question I have illustrated as far as possible from the journalism of Fielding's middle period (*c.* 1738–41). In the chapters discussing the plays, which nearly all came earlier, and the novels, which of course were later, I have tried to develop the various points I am concerned with by means of quotations which closely parallel those previously given from the journalistic writings. In other words I have shown the continuity of Fielding's moral interest implicitly rather than explicitly.

No attempt is made here to evaluate the plays, the journalism or the minor narrative works. They are considered almost entirely for their illustration of tendencies in Fielding's writing which were to be important to his development as a novelist. My concern is with the three major novels. I want to discuss how they came to be the kind of works they are, and how they function for the modern reader.

The main substance of this book was originally an Oxford B.Litt. thesis. The additions—most notably the final chapter—grow largely from my reading of E. H. Gombrich's

Art and Illusion. I hope I have not misrepresented any of Professor Gombrich's ideas in translating them from art to literature.

I would like to thank Jonathan Wordsworth of Exeter College, Oxford, for helpful suggestions about the structure of the book. I would also like to thank my wife, without whose help it would not have been completed for at least another year.

MICHAEL IRWIN

Smith College, July 1966

NOTE ON WORKS CITED

The following abbreviations have been used:

ELH	*Journal of English Literary History*
MLN	*Modern Language Notes*
MLQ	*Modern Language Quarterly*
N and Q	*Notes and Queries*
PQ	*Philological Quarterly*
PMLA	*Publications of the Modern Language Association of America*
RES	*The Review of English Studies*

As many of the quotations from Fielding's work are very brief I have made the footnotes as precise as possible by referring to the volume and page number of the Henley edition, which includes virtually all Fielding's important work. But since there is a full and scholarly edition of *The Covent-Garden Journal* (ed. Gerard Edward Jensen, New Haven and London, 1915, 2 vols.), containing material not to be found in Henley, I have also made use of that. For the benefit of readers who cannot get hold of the Henley edition I have added, after each quotation from the novels, the book and chapter number found in all editions.

Where Cross is cited in the footnotes the reference is to *The History of Henry Fielding*, by W. L. Cross, New Haven, 1918, 3 vols. When referring to *The Spectator*, I give the number of the issue according to the Everyman edition (ed. G. Gregory Smith, London and New York, 1907, 4 vols.).

CONTENTS

I

INTRODUCTION

THIS book will try to show how Fielding's novels became what they are. It rests on two assumptions: first, that it is possible to find out a great deal about what Fielding was trying to do in the novels, and how he was trying to do it; second, that, since he was building up a new literary form by trial and error, an examination of his technical successes and failures will reveal something about the potentialities of the novel in general.

The first of these assumptions probably requires more explanation than the second. Fielding's intentions as a novelist, then, are unusually clear, partly because he so often states them explicitly, partly because his entire career as a writer shows such a marked uniformity of general purpose.

The curious notion that Fielding was a genial libertine, a notion which persisted well into the present century, until finally disposed of by Cross, naturally tended to obscure the obvious fact that he is above all an ethical writer. By now, of course, this ethical concern has been generally recognized, and critics have even begun to point out that the novels have a specifically moral intention. Professor Sherburn claims that *Amelia*, at least, is so much a didactic work that 'enunciation of ethical principles pre-occupies the author rather more than plot, character, or dramatic effect';[1] M. C. Battestin has shown that the meaning and structure of *Joseph Andrews* are similarly dependent on a moral purpose.[2]

As yet, however, there have been no attempts at a comprehensive account of this aspect of Fielding's work, merely observations about particular novels. Only if his

[1] George Sherburn, 'Fielding's Social Outlook', *Eighteenth-Century English Literature*, ed. J. L. Clifford, New York and London, 1959, p. 265.
[2] In *The Moral Basis of Fielding's Art*, Middletown, Connecticut, 1959.

dramatic and journalistic writings are taken into consideration does it become possible to understand the full nature and
scope of his didactic purpose. Perhaps it would be as well at
the outset to deny the view, sometimes advanced, that these
works are 'unjustly neglected'. As far as their intrinsic
merits are concerned the neglect is very reasonable. Taken
together, though, they do have value for what they reveal of
Fielding's thought in the years prior to his first novel. They
establish, beyond question, the intensity and continuity of
his moral preoccupation. Certain didactic themes recur
again and again, introduced regularly into the plays,
expounded directly in editorial articles and occasional essays.
And these are the same themes which are eventually to become the basis of the novels. This book will isolate and
classify these themes, with a view to showing just how important they are to Fielding's work.

It will be shown that even his lighter dramas contain an
important moral element. In some of the plays he introduces
extraneous episodes solely to make a didactic point. Even in
an amoral artificial comedy he will invoke realistic ethical
standards. Regularly, in fact, Fielding's moral intention
takes precedence over the demands of form.

It is hardly surprising, then, that in the novels, where he is
free to develop his own form, the didactic purpose is an
important shaping factor. As Sherburn and Battestin suggest, and as the following chapters will show in greater
detail, each of the narratives is tailored to meet the demands
of a moral plan.

Failure to realize this fact is one of several reasons behind
the frequent misunderstanding of Fielding's work. It has
been rightly acknowledged that the new medium he evolved
was a synthesis of techniques borrowed from existing
genres: the picaresque tale, the occasional essay, the artificial
comedy. But it has been wrongly assumed that the nature of
this synthesis was determined chiefly by aesthetic considera-
tions. Fielding did have theoretical ideas about the requirements of prose narrative, of course, but his primary concern
was always didactic. His choice of techniques within the
novels was usually dictated by the cast of his moral views.
Some of them could be represented only in terms of action,

others only in terms of character. Some of them demanded a formal embodiment, some a realistic. The form Fielding developed involved an uneasy compromise between these various pressures, and can be adequately studied only with reference to them.

The chief difficulty in the way of such a study is the unaccommodating nature of Fielding's didacticism. Although his views derive from the worthiest Christian ideals, they are distinctly commonplace in themselves. Moreover they emerge less often in basic statements of principle than in a miscellany of relatively trivial observations on a variety of specific topics. They are of interest, then, almost solely for their importance to Fielding's imaginative work; and this importance is most conveniently demonstrated in terms of the frequency with which such minor points recur.

The difficulty for the critic, however, is only methodological. The ideas concerned *can* be established. So too, if less precisely, can the literary influences which helped to determine the character of his novels. It is possible to indicate, at least roughly, the sources of his narrative methods.

Here a caveat is necessary. There has already been a good deal of research into Fielding's narrative theory. But the emphasis on theory has been at the expense of an understanding of his practice. In *Amelia*, after all, he tacitly abandons many of the major principles set out in *Joseph Andrews* and *Tom Jones*. There are several possible explanations for this change of policy, but the most obvious is that the chapters on the 'comi-prosai-epic' in the earlier books were basically little more than *ad hoc* self-justification. Fielding could not have helped realizing that his work bore dangerous superficial similarities to the 'Romances' he condemned.

It is not very helpful to follow Fielding's own lead by talking, in Aristotelian terms, of fable, action, and characters. These are entities which the crudest narrative writer would have difficulty in omitting. A better starting-point is a consideration of the specific techniques Fielding uses, say, to link two chapters, to recount an episode, to demonstrate some good quality in his hero. He was not, of course, inventing but assembling a new narrative language. Essentially the novel was concocted from ingredients familiar in existing

literary forms. It is possible to deduce something about
Fielding's particular choice of ingredients because his
previous work as a writer provides helpful clues, and because a good deal is known, in one way and another, about his
reading and his literary preferences.

Each of Fielding's novels, then, is a collage. A knowledge
of his literary background will show where he culled the
different bits and pieces he makes use of. A knowledge of his
didactic motives will reveal the organizing principle behind
the assembling of these various fragments. It should then be
possible to decide how far the finished work of art is a
coherent, self-consistent whole, and how far it fulfils Fielding's stated intentions. Where there is a disparity between
what he attempts and what he achieves it may well be because
he has misjudged the requirements of his emerging form.

It is not easy, however, to make a dispassionate assess-
ment of Fielding's successes and failures as an innovator.
The rather obvious programme outlined in this chapter
would surely have been carried out long ago, were it not for
three main difficulties. One of these has already been mentioned. There was clearly no possibility of making a serious
study of Fielding as long as it was assumed that he was a
bawdy writer.

In the second place his novels tend to elicit a rather
horrible stock response from British readers. The presence,
especially in *Tom Jones*, of squires and huntsmen, coaches
and inns, induces a nostalgic euphoria that blurs critical
insight and usually seeks expression in metaphors about
Old Wine and God's Fresh Air. This attitude precludes
response to the more interesting aspects of Fielding's
achievement, and explains the fact that so much of the
critical work about the novels has been trivial and miscon-
ceived. Once a critic has decided that they are 'rollicking' he
is unlikely to get much farther with them. Who would look
for tentative experiment in a 'rollicking' work?

Objective analysis of Fielding, then, requires that this
stock response be subdued. But it also demands a second, and
much more difficult, feat of suppression : the suppression of
some of the essential instincts of the novel reader. The stock
response, of course, is induced by various elements in the

narratives which happen to have acquired irrelevant emotional associations. But the account of the books given by various critics shows that this is closely linked with another reaction—the unconscious tendency to read the novels not as the uncertain, though purposeful, experimental works which they are, but as modern works *manqués*. It is easy—irrationally—to feel that Fielding was trying to write a twentieth-century novel and falling short of it in certain respects. But naturally he was doing no such thing. He was proffering different sorts of information in different ways, and for a number of distinct purposes. His hope was that each resultant 'history' would take on life in the minds of his readers—that the different kinds of information would fuse into a coherent picture of reality. Since he was a pioneer in this difficult art it would have been surprising if he had been uniformly successful. As he tries to work out his conception some parts of it—unpredictably from his own point of view—'come alive', while others fail to do so. Yet to see why, or even exactly where, this happens, is surprisingly difficult. The power of projection—the power of filling in gaps and rounding out hints—which is probably a condition of understanding any sort of art, invests the novels with a kind of life which is to some extent anachronistic and alien to their real meaning. The reader refuses, so to speak, to register all the inconsistencies of tone or narrative level which confront him. He instinctively takes up a stance which reduces the contradictions to a minimum. He forgets passages which seem irrelevant or discordant; he assigns to the characters what motive or complexity they may seem, by contemporary standards, to lack. His estimate of the nature and purpose of the novels, therefore, may be quite at variance with the author's intentions.

The references here to 'real meaning' and 'the author's intentions' are critical shorthand, not attempts to beg any questions. Clearly a reader can be 'right' about the novels and Fielding 'wrong'. And in any case this disparity between intention and achievement afflicts many, perhaps all, works of art. The point in this case is that since Fielding was trying to build up a new medium from scratch, the reader's automatic tendency to help him out imaginatively, to assist

in the illusion, may lead him to respond irrelevantly to
aspects of the narrative of which the author is not fully in
control. It is possible to read a largely subjective life into his
books.

A roughly comparable error has been attributed to certain
of the adverse critics of *Paradise Lost*. It is said that they react
to God and Satan too much as if they were characters in a
novel, to be judged by twentieth-century standards of right
and wrong. Whether this particular charge is true is another
matter, but certainly this is a possible, and perhaps even to
some extent an unavoidable, kind of error. Generally speak-
ing, the modern reader will learn to understand a work from
the point of view of the age in which it was written, only after
he has already enjoyed it from his own point of view. In
Fielding's case, of course, the gap between the instinctive
and the 'objective' reaction is relatively narrow, but it is still
a source of misunderstanding. The recent film of *Tom Jones*,
for example, though entertaining enough, represented this
easy-going view, which has by now become stereotyped.

Because they make a conscious effort to avoid the kind of
error described above, the ensuing analyses may seem
unsympathetic. It should be made clear at once, therefore,
that this book does not aim at a total estimate of Fielding's
achievement. In any case the plays and minor writings are
referred to chiefly for the light they shed on the novels.
But even the novels are not radically reassessed. Many of
their positive qualities—their humour, their satire, their
humanity—are taken for granted. If the emphasis here very
often seems to fall on Fielding's limitations it is not in an
attempt to belittle his greatness as a writer and as a man.
E. H. Gombrich says: 'In the study of art no less than in the
study of man, the mysteries of success are frequently best
revealed through an investigation of failures.'[1] Fielding's
books have a deceptive air of simplicity. The following
chapters, by drawing attention to the frequency with which
he miscalculated, or fell into contradictions, will try to suggest how much invention and good judgement was needed

[1] *Art and Illusion*, London, 1960, p. 67. I hope it is apparent that some of
the arguments and formulations in this chapter owe a great deal to Professor
Gombrich's book.

to make his novels the works of art they are. But the account of the books given here cannot, and is not intended to, stand on its own. It is designed not to supersede the traditional account of the novels, but to be superimposed on it, amending it only in a few important respects.

II

FIELDING'S MORAL POSITION

M UCH of the thought of eighteenth-century England
involved a fundamental ambiguity. Reason was
confidently proposed as the sole arbiter of conduct,
but there remained an instinctive confidence in traditions and
beliefs originally derived from Authority. The result was a
series of compromises.

Since English society at the time was predominantly
Christian, philosophical, moral, and even political theory
were largely subsumed under religious thought. And in that
crucial sphere the tendency towards compromise was
particularly marked. Deism, one logical conclusion of a
purely rational approach to theology, created controversy but
made few converts, and was nearly forgotten by the middle of
the century. Militant atheism remained almost unheard of.
The general attitude of the Church was epitomized by the
willingness of Locke, the thinker most influential in the
period, to accept the authority both of pure intellect and of
the Bible. This partial reliance on dogma meant that the
change in contemporary Anglicanism was limited to one of
emphasis.

None the less the change was an important one. The new
belief in the capacity of the unassisted intellect to find the
way to salvation had several notable corollaries. The Deity
had to be deducible merely from the observation of external
phenomena; hence the concept of Natural Religion. Since
intellectual abilities vary, the beliefs necessary for salvation
were reduced to a few fundamentals: Locke suggested that
an acknowledgement that Christ was the Messiah was the
only essential article of Faith, all the rest stemming from it.
But since the heathen is denied any tidings about Revelation, salvation for him had in justice to be obtainable through
good deeds alone.

The general trend, then, was to reduce Christianity to a few basic imperatives. Revelation and the supernatural element were much less stressed. Works were considered far more important than faith.

These attitudes, which reflected the wide current reliance on the individual intelligence, were most systematically advanced by the latitudinarian divines. All such preachers were essentially rationalistic in their approach, South, for example, contending that 'all Arguments whatsoever against Experience are fallacious.'[1] Tillotson states: 'Nothing ought to be received as a revelation from God which plainly contradicts the principles of natural religion.'[2] It is repeatedly emphasized that virtue is natural to man, and the practice of it the only way to salvation. Tillotson goes so far as to say: 'A right faith is wholly in order to a good life, and is of no value any farther than it hath an influence upon it.'[3] The latitudinarians accept the logic of this position by stating categorically that the virtuous heathen will be saved.

Virtue itself they equate with Charity, which arises from an instinctive sympathy with the joys and sorrows of one's fellow man and a desire to assist him. Barrow asserts that there have always been many charitable persons ' ... heartily desiring the publick good, and compassionating the evils of mankind, ready with their best endeavours to procure and promote the one, to prevent and remove the other ... '[4] Such a benevolent disposition is called 'Good-nature' by several of the latitudinarians, and the term came into general use. *The Spectator*, for instance, devotes two articles to a consideration of 'Good-nature'.[5]

Since charitable actions spring from a natural sympathy, it follows that performing them will give pleasure. The idea, common to the latitudinarians, is aptly summed up by Isaac Barrow:

---

[1] Robert South, *Thirty Six Sermons and Discourses*, 5th ed., Dublin, 1720, i.2.

[2] Quoted by Leslie Stephen, *English Thought in the Eighteenth Century*, London, 1876, i.78.

[3] Quoted by Battestin, *The Moral Basis of Fielding's Art*, p. 20.

[4] *The Works of Isaac Barrow*, London, 1741, ii.83.

[5] In nos. 169 and 177.

... Nature ... hath ... made the Communication of Benefits to others, to be accompanied with a very delicious Relish upon the Mind of him that practises it; nothing indeed carrying with it a more pure and savory Delight than Beneficence. A man may be VIRTUOUSLY VOLUPTUOUS, AND A LAUDABLE EPICURE BY DOING MUCH GOOD.[1]

An emphasis on charity and an avoidance of dogma, then, were the chief characteristics of the latitudinarians. But it must be admitted that the group cannot be very rigidly defined. Although they provided much of the Christian argument in the Deist controversy they had in fact a great deal in common with their opponents. Both sides believed in the existence of a Deity, in Natural Virtue, and in the priority of Reason. Argument centred chiefly on the extent to which divine inscrutability should be invoked. Latitudinarianism is really nothing more than the Church of England formulation of the contemporary tolerance and rationalism.

But again, since England was very much an Anglican country, it was probably the latitudinarian influence which did most to condition the public attitude to Christianity and morality in the first half of the eighteenth century. At least until the advent of Whitefield and Wesley the dogmatic and mystical sides of religion were very much subordinated to the moral side. The sermons of the Low Church divines show one effect of the new system of priorities. As compared with the homilies of the previous century they are much less formal in tone, much less grandiloquent and doctrinaire. They are written to appeal directly to the intelligence of the ordinary educated man. It was no doubt this lowering of tone which helped to encourage the notable increase in secular moral writing at the beginning of the eighteenth century; the language of didacticism had moved much closer to that of everyday cultivated speech. Soon *The Tatler* and *The Spectator* were making literary and commercial capital out of stylish moralizing and elegant admonishment. By the time Fielding came to write, an ethical intention was essential to any serious writer and open exhortation was a commonplace.

---

[1] Quoted in *The Covent-Garden Journal*, i.308.

I

M. C. Battestin, in his recent study of *Joseph Andrews*, claims that 'Fielding's ethic has been traced to its source in the popular latitudinarianism of his day.'[1] If he is implying that Fielding's beliefs were specifically derived from the Low Church homilists he is over-simplifying the issue. Many of their attitudes—as was indicated above—were generally current, and shared even by the Deists. It is impossible, therefore, despite a number of verbal parallels, to tell when Fielding is drawing particularly upon the latitudinarians' work, and when merely expressing a widely-accepted view which they happen to share.

None the less he was clearly an admirer of the Low Church homilists. His library contained the works of Chillingworth, South, Barrow, Clarke, and Tillotson. In *The Champion* he claims that the two last have amply demonstrated 'the immortality of the soul, and the certainty of a future state'.[2] In the poem *Of True Greatness* he extols Hoadly;[3] and regularly in his journalism he quotes South, whom he praises as wittier than Congreve,[4] and above all 'our favourite Dr. Barrow'. Like the latitudinarians he is opposed to the misanthropic pessimism of Hobbes and Mandeville,[5] and to the Deists' denial of Revelation and of the life to come.[6] He uses the argument previously employed by Tillotson, South, and Barrow, among others, by which earthly suffering is made evidence of a future existence.[7]

But from the point of view of his imaginative writing by far the most significant attitude he shares with the latitudinarians is a belief in the paramount importance of Charity. In *An Inquiry into the Causes of the Late Increase in Robbers* he asserts: 'Indeed the passion of love or benevolence ... seems to be the only human passion that is in itself simply and absolutely good ... '[8] Regularly in his works he uses the term 'Good-nature' in a sense similar to that in which it is employed by the homilists. It is worth quoting Fielding's

---

[1] *The Moral Basis of Fielding's Art*, p. 11.
[2] Henley ed., xv.163.   [3] Henley ed., xii.256.
[4] *The Covent-Garden Journal*, i.243.   [5] (e.g.) Henley ed., xv.94, 165 ff.
[6] (e.g.) Henley ed., xv.161 ff.   [7] (e.g.) Henley ed., xv.218.
[8] Henley ed., xiii.110.

own definitions of the word. That in *The Champion* has close affinities with Barrow's comment on charity quoted above: 'Good-nature is a delight in the happiness of mankind, and a concern at their misery, with a desire, as much as possible, to procure the former, and avert the latter; and this, with a constant regard to desert.'[1] There is a similar statement in *An Essay on the Knowledge of the Characters of Men*:

> Good-nature is that benevolent and amiable temper of mind, which disposes us to feel the misfortunes, and enjoy the happiness of others; and, consequently, pushes us on to promote the latter, and prevent the former; and that without any abstract contemplation on the beauty of virtue, and without the allurements or terrors of religion.[2]

The qualifications to these definitions are not important. In the first example Fielding is concerned to establish the necessity for discrimination since he is to go on to suggest that bringing a criminal to justice 'is, perhaps, the best natured office we can perform to society'. In the second he wishes to make it clear that the feeling in question is natural and spontaneous. A third definition, in the poem *Of Good-nature*, is limited to the essential qualities:

> What by this name, then, shall be understood?
> What? but the glorious lust of doing good?
> The heart that finds its happiness to please
> Can feel another's pain, and taste his ease;
> The cheek that with another's joy can glow,
> Turn pale and sicken with another's woe . . . [3]

These definitions are not, however, of great practical significance. In *The Champion* Fielding says: 'I do not know a better general definition of virtue, than that it is a delight in doing good . . . '[4] Good-nature for him, then, as for the latitudinarians, is practically synonymous with virtue itself, and merely provides a convenient label for the warm and active sympathy which he regards as the foundation of all morality.

[1] Henley ed., xv.258.
[2] Henley ed., xiv.285.
[3] Henley ed., xii.258–9.
[4] Henley ed., xv.136.

The use of the word 'delight' in two of these descriptions suggests that incentive to the benevolent disposition which Fordyce was to call 'Self-approving Joy'.[1] Fielding quotes Barrow's passage on Christian epicureanism in The Covent-Garden Journal and frequently advances the same idea in his own terms: '. . . what can give greater Happiness to a good Mind, than the Reflexion on having relieved the Misery or contributed to the well being, of his Fellow-Creature.'[2] Vice, on the other hand, being antipathetic to man's natural moral sense, must ultimately cause uneasiness, as Fielding suggests in the Preface to the Miscellanies: 'The same righteous judge [= conscience] always annexes a bitter anxiety to the purchases of guilt, whilst it adds a double sweetness to the enjoyments of innocence and virtue . . . '[3] Regularly the corollary is stressed:

. . . if we strip virtue and vice of all their outward ornaments and appearances, and view them both naked . . . we shall, I trust, find virtue to have in her every thing that is truly valuable, to be a constant mistress, a faithful friend, and a pleasant companion; while vice will appear a tawdry, painted harlot, within, all foul and impure, enticing only at a distance, the possession of her certainly attended with uneasiness, pain, disease, poverty, and dishonour.[4]

These few basic ideas on charity, constantly expressed and re-expressed in Fielding's work, constitute what might be called the positive side of his didactic beliefs. But although frequently at pains to propagate these constructive moral views, he is more often, and more characteristically, a satirist. His simple precept of active charitableness becomes significant in his writings partly because of the host of negative attitudes it implies.

Since Fielding's cardinal virtues are kindness and concern for others, his cardinal sins are naturally cruelty and egotism. He concludes an attack on 'roasting' in The Champion:

If we consider this diversion in the worst light, it will appear to be no other than a delight in seeing the miseries, misfortunes, and frailties

[1] Quoted by R. S. Crane, 'Genealogy of the Man of Feeling', ELH, i. (1934), 205.
[2] The Covent-Garden Journal, ii.9.　　　[3] Henley ed., xii.244.
[4] The Champion, Henley ed., xv.167.

of mankind displayed; and a pleasure and joy conceived in their sufferings therein. A pleasure, perhaps, as inhuman, and which must arise from a nature as thoroughly corrupt and diabolical, as can possibly pollute the mind of man.[1]

Fielding often stresses his high regard for women; his sexual ethic, therefore, is less concerned with abstract notions of chastity than with an insistence that the woman must not be made a victim of treachery:

This Letter is designed for the Use of the loveliest, and, I sincerely think, the best Part of the Creation, who seldom stray but when they are misled by Men; by whom they are deceived, corrupted, betrayed, and often *brought to Destruction, both of Body and Soul*. In the Sequel therefore, I will treat in general of these Corrupters of the Innocence of Women; and of the extreme Baseness as well as Cruelty of this Practice, how favourably soever the World may please to receive it.[2]

Similarly it is because of the slaughter and misery that they cause that 'Great Men' are often the object of Fielding's satire. Even ill-treatment of animals is attacked in a special article in *The Champion*.[3] Fielding could tolerate no form of cruelty.

For him the types of egotism are the avaricious and the ambitious man. He condemns miserliness more often and more virulently than any other single vice. In *The Champion*, to quote an obvious instance, two whole editorials are given up to a dream-vision satirizing avarice.[4] A certain amount of ambition Fielding is prepared to tolerate; he says of Virtue that: 'Ambition itself, if moderate, she will countenance, she will not indeed permit you, by all means whatever, to rise and advance yourself; yet she has been known to raise some to the highest dignities in the State, in the Army, and in the Law.'[5] When he attacks ambition, which is frequently, it is on the assumption that it is shameless and unscrupulous, as in the case of the ruthless general, the fawning courtier, or the crafty politician.

Yet that the miser and the self-seeker frequently thrive, and enjoy a good reputation in the world, is a fact Fielding

---

[1] Henley ed., xv.243.
[2] *The Covent-Garden Journal*, i.255.
[3] Henley ed., xv.252 ff.
[4] Henley ed., xv.121 ff.
[5] *The Champion*, Henley ed., xv.167.

cannot gainsay. He attributes their success to a capacity for acting one part and playing another. Hypocrisy, therefore, becomes an important and recurrent target. In *The Champion* he publishes what purports to be a letter from a hypocrite:

> My temper is so far from being inclined to good nature, that I always triumph in other people's misfortunes, yet, at the expense of a little verbal pity ... I pass for a very good-natured person ... you already, I believe, conclude that I have a heart not too charitably disposed; and yet I am the only person of my acquaintance who will tell you that I am not the most charitable creature alive; for though I never give any thing myself, yet I always abuse others for not giving more.[1]

Fielding was not alone in thinking that the virtuous man was particularly vulnerable to this kind of dissimulation on the part of the vicious.[2] He complains in *The Champion*:

> Honest and undesigning men of very good understanding would be always liable to the attacks of cunning and artful knaves, into whose snares we are as often seduced by the openness and goodness of the heart, as by the weakness of the head. True wisdom is commonly attended with a simplicity of manners, which betrays a worthy man to a tricking shuffler, of a much inferior capacity.[3]

It was to protect the ingenuous that he wrote *An Essay on the Knowledge of the Characters of Men*, which was designed to show how to detect a man's true disposition by careful observation. More generally, in nearly all his works he strives to unmask affectation and deceit. Much of his best writing defends real, as against professed, ethical standards.

If these various aspects of conduct with which Fielding occupies himself have a common denominator it is that they all involve behaviour between people; his chief didactic concern was social morality. This fact has an important implication for his imaginative writing. As the various vices and virtues he is to depict are essentially those of everyday life, they can only be fully realized in drama or fiction if the context is reasonably close to common experience. Thus the

---

[1] Henley ed., xv.95.   [2] Cf. *The Spectator*, no. 245.
[3] Henley ed., xv.217.

fulfilment of Fielding's didactic purpose demands a large degree of realism.

2

Because Fielding was a very practical moralist he naturally tended to attack particular evils visible in society. Explicit and detailed social criticism was already a literary commonplace. Although much of the didactic content of *The Tatler* and *The Spectator* is confined to gentle satire against the affectations of fashionable life, there is an underlying awareness of 'that desperate State of Vice and Folly into which the Age is fallen'.[1] The Spectator often censures the manners and morals of the day with real severity; and he makes a host of particular criticisms. He condemns duelling, 'wenching', and the degeneracy of the stage. He attacks the empty life of the town, and the fatuity of masquerades and Italian opera.[2]

The nature and the effectiveness of these criticisms are aptly summarized in Gay's well-known comment on Steele:

> There is this noble difference between him and all the rest of our polite and gallant authors: the latter have endeavoured to please the age by falling in with them, and encouraging them in their fashionable vices and false notions of things . . . Bickerstaff ventured to tell the town that they were a parcel of fops, fools and vain coquettes; but in such a manner as even pleased them, and made them more than half inclined to believe that he spoke truth.[3]

Gay himself indulges in similar social criticism, and he often shows genuine bitterness in his moral satire:

> That wretch, to gain an equipage and place,
> Betray'd his sister to a lewd embrace.
> This coach, that with the blazon'd 'scutcheon glows,
> Vain of his unknown race, the coxcomb shows.
> Here the brib'd lawyer, sunk in velvet, sleeps;
> The starving orphan, as he passes, weeps . . . [4]

---

[1] *The Spectator*, no. 10; Everyman ed., i.38.

[2] (e.g.) *The Spectator*, nos. 8, 97, 182, 446.

[3] Quoted in the Introduction to *The Tatler*, ed. G. A. Aitken, London, 1898, i.xvii.

[4] 'Trivia' ii.575 ff., *The Poetical Works of John Gay*, ed. G. C. Faber, London, 1926, p. 78.

These lines illustrate Gay's constant awareness of the separation of merit and material reward. Everywhere in fashionable life vices were flourishing which would be punished among the poor. He sums up the injustice in *Polly*:

> All crimes are judg'd like fornication;
>> While rich we are honest no doubt.
> Fine ladies can keep reputation,
>> Poor lasses alone are found out.
> If justice had piercing eyes,
>> Like ourselves to look within,
> She'd find power and wealth a disguise
> That shelter the worst of our kin.[1]

The Beggar's Opera is substantially an ironic expansion of the same idea.

It is unlikely that Fielding was influenced by any of these writers in regard to the matter of his moralizing. Their work is cited here partly to show that he had ample precedent in the sphere of social criticism, and partly to illustrate a widespread conviction in the period that contemporary life was riddled with triviality, corruption and injustice. The culminating expression of this disgust, Brown's *Estimate*, was not published until 1757. Virtually throughout Fielding's life, therefore, Vice and Folly were considered to be rife, and perhaps increasingly so. As a practical moralist he could hardly fail to perceive the many specific symptoms of degeneracy and condemn what he thought to be its causes.

It is important to an understanding of Fielding's social views to realize that he believed the immorality of the age to be very closely linked with its folly. In *A Charge to the Grand Jury*, for instance, he states the connexion:

Gentlemen, our newspapers, from the top of the page to the bottom, the corners of our streets up to the very eaves of our houses, present us with nothing but a view of masquerades, balls, and assemblies of various kinds, fairs, wells, gardens, &c., tending to promote idleness, extravagance, and immorality, among all sorts of people.

This fury after licentious and luxurious pleasures is grown to so enormous a height, that it may be called the characteristic of the present age. And it is an evil, gentlemen, of which it is neither easy nor pleasant to foresee all the consequences.[2]

[1] Ibid., p. 585.   [2] Henley ed., xiii.214–15.

Fielding's constant satire against particular and often trivial
social targets represents, then, more than an idiosyncratic
personal animus. Much of even his lightest satire stems
from this fundamental conviction that the follies of society
are tending to corrupt the nation's morals. Hence the
repeated attacks on beaux, for example:

> The rotten beau, while smell'd along the room,
> Divides your nose 'twixt stenches and perfume . . . [1]

or on 'the wild coquette, and the censorious prude'.[2] The
pastimes of society are also condemned; the drums and masquerades, the card-parties and ridottos, the Italian opera and
the puerile theatrical entertainments.

It must be remembered that since 'the Age' to Fielding
and his contemporaries meant only current High Society,
this piecemeal criticism of manners and amusements amounts
to a fairly comprehensive denunciation. *The Spectator* gives
the diary of a rich spinster's typical week; there is a device
for trifling away every hour of the day.[3] The way of life of
many of the wealthy consisted solely of the diversions which
Fielding ridicules.

But the corruptness of the age is very often attacked
directly. In *The True Patriot* there is an indignant letter
from Parson Adams:

> Can we expect to find charity in an age, when scarce any refuse to
> own the most profligate rapaciousness! when no man is ashamed of
> avowing the pursuit of riches through every dirty road and track?
> To speak out, in an age when every thing is venal; and when there is
> scarce one among the mighty who would not be equally ashamed at
> being thought not to set *some* price on himself, as he would at being
> imagined to set too low a one?[4]

Elections, preferment, even titles can be gained by money.
Medicine and the law are corrupted, many of their practi-
tioners being mere charlatans with a smattering of jargon.
Dishonest lawyers and physicians feature again and again in

---

[1] *To John Hayes Esq.*, Henley ed., xii.275.

[2] *To a Friend*, Henley ed., xii.272.

[3] *The Spectator*, no. 323. Fielding uses the same idea in Wilson's story in
Joseph Andrews.

[4] Henley ed., xiv.28.

Fielding's work. On occasion he implies that even the Church is tainted with this materialism.[1]

The result of this venality is that virtue and merit are at a discount:

> A very virtuous man may starve in Westminster Hall, or among the fair traders in the city, while the gentleman who would take fees in any cause, or sometimes on both sides of the same cause; and the trader who swears solemnly that he gets nothing by his silk at a crown a yard, and sells it afterwards for four shillings, will be pretty sure of growing rich.[2]

In the sphere of literature 'true wit and genius' are 'in a manner deposed, and imposters advanced in their place'[3]: ' . . . for I think I may affirm with truth, that there is no one patron of true genius, nor the least encouragement left for it in this kingdom.'[4] There is a similar lack of encouragement for military merit. Fielding refers to: ' . . . an acquaintance of mine, who, after he had served many campaigns in Flanders, and been wounded in Spain, with a generous heart and an empty pocket died in the King's Bench . . . '[5] Even marriage has become a way of making money. A pretty girl is a marketable property, disposed of to the highest bidder, and must resign herself to a loveless marriage.[6] Understandably such unions frequently lapse first into hatred and then into adultery. Altogether Fielding's writings imply a society that is decadent, frivolous, and often brutal.

It is by comparison with this gloomy picture of the town that his constant ideal of a peaceful country existence gains in persuasiveness. In one of Fielding's contributions to his sister's *Familiar Letters*, a Miss Lucy Rural, having received her friend's account of the delights of the city, replies that she is: ' . . . convinced of the impertinence and stupidity of a town-life; and that we are not only more innocent, but much more merry and happy in the country.'[7] No doubt, as Battestin suggests, this theme partly derives from poetic

---

[1] (e.g.) *The Champion*, Henley ed., xv.273.
[2] *The Champion*, Henley ed., xv.172.
[3] *Familiar Letters*, Henley ed., xvi.28.
[4] *Familiar Letters*, Henley ed., xv.31.
[5] *The Champion*, Henley ed., xv.78.
[6] (e.g.) *The Champion*, Henley ed., xv.192.   [7] Henley ed., xvi.43.

tradition; but with Fielding the attitude is not purely a philosophical one. The country was preferable to the town not necessarily in absolute terms, but because the contemporary values of the town happened to be particularly vicious and inane. In any case the superior happiness of rural life is a constant theme in Fielding.

This rough categorizing of the social comments and criticisms which recur most frequently in Fielding's work probably makes them appear too unoriginal and miscellaneous to form a serious part of a didactic writer's material. But while it is true that Fielding was often repeating strictures previously passed by Steele, Gay, and others, he no doubt felt that he had an ethical justification for doing so. It was the moralist's task to be effective rather than original. Some critics have been puzzled that Fielding should find Dr. South 'wittier than Congreve'; but he was probably thinking of South's own definition: 'Wit in Divinity is nothing else, but Sacred Truths suitably expressed.'[1] Fielding shared this belief in the importance of apt new formulations of familiar ideas. He suggests as much in *An Essay on the Knowledge of the Characters of Men*:

> Neither will the reader, I hope, be offended, if he should here find no observations entirely new to him. Nothing can be plainer, or more known, than the general rules of morality, and yet thousands of men are thought well employed in reviving our remembrance, and enforcing our practice of them.[2]

Since the specific social evils he was concerned to criticize flourished throughout his life it is not surprising to find the same particular targets attacked again and again.

More notable in its effect on Fielding's work is the miscellaneousness of much of his satire. His didacticism tends to take two distinctive forms. The positive side, the propagation of the ideal of Charity, provides a constant point of reference, even when left tacit and only implied through irony. The negative side, the condemnation of various vices, and more particularly of various social practices, finds expression in a host of self-contained, usually satirical, attacks.

[1] *Thirty Six Sermons and Discourses*, ed. cit., ii.14.
[2] Henley ed., xiv.283.

It is the heterogeneousness of these attacks which is the other main factor conditioning Fielding's chosen literary forms. As the ensuing chapters will show, the multiplicity of minor didactic comment has a marked effect on the coherence and the continuity of both his dramatic and his narrative writing.

3

Since the corruptness Fielding censured extended to the political and legal administration of the times his satire naturally tended to imply flaws in the system. In his later years, when working as a magistrate, he criticized various specific weaknesses in the law. Yet it never occurs to him to question the system as a whole. He has complete faith in the current social order, and attributes any failings in it solely to the corruptness or inadequacy of individuals. For him any malaise in society can be no more than the sum total of its symptoms.

This implicit confidence in the existing order of things has a special significance for Fielding's didactic position in that he derives from it certain assumptions which do not quite square with his moral beliefs. The slight contradiction involved may be observed in some of his comments on rank. In *An Essay on Conversation* he states: 'Men are superior to each other in this our country by title, by birth, by rank in profession, and by age . . . '[1] Later in the essay he confirms his belief in birth, saying that he would not withhold from it 'that deference which the policy of government hath assigned it'.[2] But at another point he admits:

. . . birth . . . is a poor and mean pretence to honour, when supported with no other. Persons who have no better claim to superiority, should be ashamed of this; they are really a disgrace to those very ancestors from whom they would derive their pride . . . [3]

There is clearly a clash here between Fielding's acceptance of the idea that birth can confer social superiority and his practical view that superiority must depend on some kind of

[1] Henley ed., xiv.257–8.   [2] Henley ed., xiv.266.
[3] Henley ed., xiv.265.

intrinsic merit. Elsewhere his position becomes still less certain: 'The respect paid to men on account of their titles is paid at least to the supposal of their superior virtues and abilities, or it is paid to nothing.'[1] Since 'superior virtues and abilities' would be entitled to respect in any case, Fielding implies that title *per se* is a meaningless distinction.

The inconsistency to which he is tending may seem a small one, but its implications are far-reaching. In a sense his dilemma is a product of the basic intellectual ambiguity mentioned at the beginning of this chapter. Reason was made the ultimate criterion, but old forms of thought were still instinctively preserved. Hence in this case Fielding retains his belief in the validity of rank, though he can neither justify it in practical terms, nor derive it from supernatural dispensation.

The effect of this kind of uncertainty is to impair the objectivity essential to his role as moral commentator. For example in both *An Inquiry into the Causes of the Late Increase in Robbers* and *A Proposal for Making an Effectual Provision for the Poor*, he draws a distinction between the idle rich man and the idle beggar. The former is a useful member of the community because his very luxury provides employment and promotes the circulation of money. The latter, however, having only his labour to offer to society, is a useless member, and must legally be compelled to work. Similarly the rich are to be allowed their trivial entertainments, 'their masquerades and ridottos; their assemblies, drums, routs, riots, and hurricanes',[2] while the poor are to be debarred them, since in their case such pleasures are likely to lead to crime: 'In diversions, as in many other particulars, the upper part of life is distinguished from the lower.'[3] When Fielding is discussing the dispensation of charity in *The Champion*,[4] he at once excludes beggars from any benefit, because these 'deserve punishment more than relief'. The chief beneficiaries should be gentlefolk who have impoverished themselves through over-spending.

---

[1] *An Essay on Nothing*, Henley ed., xiv.316.
[2] *Inquiry*, Henley ed., xiii.27.   [3] *Inquiry*, Henley ed., xiii.28.
[4] Henley ed., xv.203 ff.